CHARLES DICKENS

A Christmas CAROL

Adapted for the stage by

Paul Sills

APPLAUSE
NEW YORK • LONDON

A Christmas Carol by Charles Dickens
Adapted by Paul Sills
© 2001 by Paul Sills
ISBN 1-55783-550-0
ALL RIGHTS RESERVED

Library of Congress Cataloging-in-Publication Data:

Sills, Paul.
    A Christmas Carol / by Charles Dickens ; adapted for the stage by Paul Sills
        p. cm.
    ISBN 1-55783-550-0
    1. Scrooge, Ebenezer (Fictitious character)--Drama. 2. London (England)
--Drama. 3. Poor families--Drama--. 4. Sick children--Drama. 5. Misers--
Drama. I. Dickens, Charles, 1812-1870. Christmas carol. II. Title.

PS3569.I449 C48 2001
812'.54--dc21

                                                        2001045129

APPLAUSE THEATRE & CINEMA BOOKS
151 W46th Street, 8th Floor
New York, NY 10036
Phone: (212) 575-9265
Fax: (646) 562-5852
email: info@applausepub.com
www.applausepub.com

COMBINED BOOK SERVICES LTD.
Units I/K, Paddock Wood
    Distribution Centre
Paddock Wood, Tonbridge,
Kent TN 12 6UU
Phone: (44) 01892 837171
Fax: (44) 01892 837272

SALES & DISTRIBUTION, HAL LEONARD CORP.
7777 West Bluemond Road, P.O. Box 13819
Milwaukee, WI 53213
Phone: (414) 774-3630 Fax: (414) 774-3259
email: halinfo@halleonard.com
internet: www.halleonard.com

INTRODUCTION

Carol and I found a century-old farm in Door County, Wisconsin in 1970, when the Broadway show was running at the Ambassador Theater. Leaving this home base from time to time we went and did story theater in the cities.

It was years before I began to direct community theater shows in Door County. Not until asked to direct a production of Charles Dickens' *A Christmas Carol* did I know what it was to work with kids and teenagers and local people with no theatrical experience.[1] Rehearsing three times a week, two hours a session, with a little extra time as performance neared, even though over a two month period, did not leave time for training the players. What helped were a few Spolin theater games.

To warm up, besides playing traditional games to bring everyone happily into the same place, I coached the troupe, children and adults together, in playing

---

[1] In my December 1994 production at the Door Community Auditorium in Fish Creek, Gerald Pelrine was Producer and Scrooge. The other adults in the cast were Richard Engberg, Martha Garvey, John Redmann, Bruce McKeefry, Jeanne Aurelius, Leif Erickson, Valerie Murre, Debbra Mahlzahn, Rich Higdon, Dan Beck, David Hatch; teenagers: Claude Cote, Ali Rericha, Neva Sills, Adrian Murre, Alisson Burda; children: Kate Fordney, Nathan Hatch, Martha Aurelius, and Christina Fordney as Tiny Tim. Music was by Fred Kaz, longtime pianist for Second City; stage design by Carol Bleackley; costumes by Joan Kelly and Polly Sills; stage manager, Barbara Fordney.

Viola Spolin's Feeling Self With Self and in her Space Walks, which take very little time. For speech I did Vowels and Consonants on the text or in small group conversations, and Extended Sound, where players send sound through space to fellow players, and let it land, then begin to focus on the sound in words.

The theater games that follow were written by Viola Spolin when she was special consultant for my production of Ovid's Metamophoses[2] at the Mark Taper Forum in Los Angeles.

In editing A Christmas Carol for the theater, I tried to stay with what Dickens the storyteller wanted us to hear. At no time did I dramatize a scene but always kept to his narrative, only eliminating the occasional digression. For Dickens has something to say to us but knows that before we can hear him we must come to heartbreak, and he brings it about. By narrative means he helps us to experience the joy of repentance. A Scottish philosopher, Thomas Carlyle, who did not keep Christmas, on reading A Christmas Carol sent out for a turkey and asked two friends to dine. Jane Welsh Carlyle wrote that her husband "was seized with a perfect convulsion of hospitality" and "actually insisted on improvising two dinner parties with only a day in between."

---

2 *Ovid's Metamorphoses*, adapted with Arnold Weinstein, will be published by Applause Books in a companion volume, along with *The Wind in the Willows* by Kenneth Grahame, *Monkey* by Wu Cheng En, and *The American Revolution, Part One*.

CHARLES DICKENS'

A CHRISTMAS CAROL

Stave one:
Marley's Ghost

Stave Two: Christmas Past
The First of the Three Spirits

Intermission

Stave Three: Christmas Present
The Second of the Three Spirits

Stave Four: Christmas Past
The Last of the Great Spirits

Stave Five:
The End of It

Characters

Bob Cratchit
Ebenezer Scrooge
Fred
Solicitor
Solicitor
Marley's Ghost
The Waiter
The Ghost of Christmas Past
Youngest Scrooge
Young Scrooge
Little Fan
Schoolmaster
Servant
Postboy
Dick Wilkins
Fezziwig
Mrs. Fezziwig
Miss Fezziwig
Belle
Ghost of Christmas Present
Six Shipmates
Mrs. Cratchit
Belinda Cratchit
Peter Cratchit
Martha Cratchit
Boy Cratchit
Girl Cratchit
Tiny Tim

(Twenty-two players, including four under the age of twelve.)

ACT I

STAVE ONE: MARLEY'S GHOST

SLIDE No. 1, FOGGY LONDON. (Fog machine is on, black traveller is open to the width of the projection. Stave sign is brought on and hung, s.r.or s.l.)

(A Young Person's chorus sing 'God Rest Ye Merry Gentlemen' and hold out the hat before the door, which is space, to Scrooge's office, downstage center. Cratchit comes to work and gives them a coin; Scrooge comes and gestures them to 'Go away!')

CHORUS ONE. Once upon a time - of all the good days in the year, on Christmas Eve - it was cold, bleak, biting weather: foggy withal.

CHORUS TWO. The people went wheezing up and down, beating their hands upon their breasts,

CHORUS THREE. and stamping their feet upon the pavement stones to warm them.

CHORUS FOUR. The fog came pouring in at every chink and keyhole,

CHORUS FIVE. the houses opposite were mere phantoms.

SCROOGE. The door of Scrooge's counting-house was open that he might keep his eye upon his clerk,

CRATCHIT. who in a dismal little cell beyond, a sort of tank, was copying letters.

SCROOGE. Scrooge had a very small fire,

CRATCHIT. but the clerk's fire was so very much smaller that it looked like one coal. But he couldn't replenish it,

SCROOGE. for Scrooge kept the coal-box in his own room.

CRATCHIT. Wherefore the clerk *(puts on long scarf)* tried to warm himself at the candle. *(he fails)*

CHORUS ONE. Oh! but he was a tight-fisted hand at the grindstone, Scrooge!

CHORUS TWO. A squeezing, wrenching, grasping,

CHORUS THREE. scraping, clutching,

CHORUS FOUR. covetous old sinner!

CHORUS FIVE. Hard and sharp as flint;

CHORUS THREE. secret and self-contained,

CHORUS ONE. and solitary as an oyster.

FRED. *(entering)* A merry Christmas, Uncle! God save you! It was Scrooge's nephew, Fred.

SCROOGE. *(startled)* Bah! Humbug!

FRED. Christmas as humbug, Uncle! You don't mean that, I am sure?

SCROOGE. I do. Merry Christmas! What right have you to be merry? What reason have you to be merry? You're poor enough.

FRED. *(gaily)* Come then. What right have you to be dismal? What reason have you to be morose? You're rich enough.

SCROOGE. Bah! Humbug!

FRED. Don't be cross, Uncle.

SCROOGE. What else can I be when I live in such a world of fools as this? Merry Christmas! Out upon Merry Christmas! What's Christmas time to you but a time for paying bills without money; a time for finding yourself a year older, and not an hour richer. If I could work my will, every idiot who goes about with 'Merry Christmas' on his lips should be boiled with his own pudding, and buried with a stake of holly through his heart.

FRED. *(pleading)* Uncle!

SCROOGE. Nephew! Keep Christmas in your own way, and let me keep it in mine.

FRED. Keep it! But you don't keep it.

SCROOGE. Let me leave it alone then. Much good may it do you! Much good it has ever done you.

FRED. There are many things, by which I have not profited, I dare say, Christmas among the rest. But I am sure I have always thought of Christmas time, when it has come round, as a good time: the only time I know of, in the long calendar of the year, when men and women seem to open their shut-up hearts freely, and to think of other people as if they really were fellow-passengers to the grave, and not another race of creatures bound on other journeys. And therefore, Uncle, though it has never put a scrap of gold or silver in my pocket, I believe that it *has* done me good, and *will* do me good; and I say, God bless it!

(Cratchit involuntarily applauds; then aware of the impropriety, pokes the fire, extinguishing it.)

SCROOGE. Let me hear another sound from *you*, and you'll keep your Christmas by losing your situation. *(turning to Fred)* You're quite a powerful speaker, sir. I wonder you don't go into Parliament.

FRED. Don't be angry, Uncle. Come! Dine with us to-morrow.

SCROOGE. I'll see you in hell first.

FRED. But why? Why?

SCROOGE. Why did you get married?

FRED. Because I fell in love.

SCROOGE. Because you fell in love. Good afternoon!

FRED. Nay, Uncle, but you never came to see me before that happened. Why give it as a reason for not coming now?

SCROOGE. Good afternoon.

FRED. I am sorry, with all my heart, to find you so resolute. But I'll keep my Christmas humor to the last. So A Merry Christmas, Uncle!

SCROOGE. Good afternoon!

FRED. And a Happy New Year!

SCROOGE. Good afternoon!

(Fred leaves the room, stops to bestow season's greetings on the clerk, who, cold as he is, returns them cordially.)

SCROOGE. There's another fellow, my clerk, with fifteen shillings a week, and a wife and family, talking about a merry Christmas. I'll retire to Bedlam.

(As Fred exits, he lets in two pleasant looking people who carry books and papers, and bow to Scrooge.)

ONE. At this festive season of the year, Mr. Scrooge, *(taking up a pen)* it is more than usually desirable to make some slight provision for the poor and destitute, who suffer greatly at the present time. Many thousands are in want of common necessaries;

TWO. Hundreds of thousands are in want of common comforts, sir.

SCROOGE. Are there no prisons?

TWO. Plenty of prisons.

SCROOGE. And the Union workhouses? Are they still in operation?

ONE. They are. Still, I wish I could say they were not.

SCROOGE. The Treadmill and the Poor Law are in full vigor, then?

ONE. Both very busy, sir.

SCROOGE. Oh! I was afraid from what you said at first that something had stopped them. I'm very glad to hear it.

TWO. They scarcely furnish Christian cheer of mind or body. A few of us are raising a fund to buy the Poor some meat and drink, and means of warmth.

ONE. We choose this time because it is a time when Want is keenly felt, and Abundance rejoices. What shall I put you down for?

SCROOGE. Nothing!

ONE. You wish to be anonymous?

SCROOGE. I wish to be left alone. Since you ask me what I wish, that is my answer. I don't make merry myself at Christmas, and I can't afford to make idle people merry. I help to support the establishments I have mentioned: they cost enough: and those who are badly off must go there.

TWO. Many can't go there; and many would rather die.

SCROOGE. If they would rather die, they had better do it, and decrease the surplus population. Good afternoon.

(Seeing it is useless to pursue their point the two withdraw, leaving Scrooge to resume his labors in a better mood. As the two are leaving, a boy looks in and sings to him:)

BOY. 'God bless you merry gentlemen, Let nothing you dismay'...

(Scrooge seizes a ruler and attacks, the boy flees.)

CRATCHIT. *(hearing bells)* At length the hour of shutting up the counting-house arrived.

SCROOGE. With an ill-will Scrooge dismounted from his stool.

(Seeing his tacit admission of the fact, the clerk instantly snuffs his candle and puts on his hat.)

SCROOGE. You'll want all day tomorrow, I suppose.

CRATCHIT. If quite convenient, sir.

SCROOGE. It's not convenient, and it's not fair. If I was to stop half-a-crown for it, you'd think yourself ill used, I'll be bound?

CRATCHIT. The clerk smiled faintly.

SCROOGE. And yet, you don't think *me* ill used, when I pay a day's wages for no work.

CRATCHIT. The clerk observed that it was only once a year.

SCROOGE. A poor excuse for picking a man's pocket every twenty-fifth of December. *(He buttons his great-coat to the chin.)* But I suppose you must have the whole day. Be here all the earlier next morning!

CRATCHIT. The clerk promised that he would.

(Scrooge walks out with a growl. The clerk closes the

office in a twinkling and, with his long comforter dangling, he has no great-coat, he rushes out.)

(A group of children run in playing, going to slide down a hill.)

CRATCHIT. In honor of its being Christmas eve, the clerk got behind a line of children, and went down a slide twenty times, and then ran home as hard as he could pelt to play at blindman's-buff. *(Exeunt omnes, projection off, traveller closes.)*

SCROOGE. *(a waiter brings out a chair and sets it as at a space table)* Scrooge took his melancholy dinner in his usual melancholy tavern; and having read all the newspapers, and beguiled the rest of the evening with his bankbook *(space objects)*, went home to bed. He lived in a house that had once belonged to his deceased partner. It was dreary enough, for nobody lived in it but Scrooge, the other rooms being all let out as offices. The yard was so dark that even Scrooge had to grope with his hands. Now, it is a fact, that there was nothing at all particular about the knocker on the door, except that it was very large. And then let anyone explain to me how it happened that Scrooge *(his key in the lock)* saw in the knocker, not a knocker but Marley's face.

MARLEY'S FACE. Marley's face. It had a dismal light about it, like a bad lobster in a dark cellar. It was not angry or ferocious, but looked at Scrooge with ghostly spectacles turned up upon its ghostly forehead. *(The hair seems to blow in a wind, the eyes are perfectly motionless)*

SCROOGE. *(As Scrooge looks fixedly)* It was a knocker again. To say that he was not startled would be untrue. *(But he puts the key in the lock, turns the door; examines back of door and sees nothing but the screws)* Pooh, pooh! Nobody under the table, *(Bed and bed-curtains enter)*nobody under the sofa, nobody under the bed, nobody in the closet. He double-locked himself in. There was a clanking noise deep down below, as if some person were dragging a heavy chain in the wine-merchant's cellar. *(A booming sound, then a chain on the stairs)* It's humbug still! I won't believe it. It came on through the heavy door, and passed into the room before his eyes. The dying flame leaped up as though it cried:

FLAME. I know him! Marley's Ghost!

(The Ghost is wrapped in chains, its jaw bound with a kerchief.)

SCROOGE. *(cold and caustic, as ever)* How now! What do you want with me!

MARLEY. Much!

SCROOGE. Marley's voice, no doubt about it. Who are you?

MARLEY. Ask me who I *was*.

SCROOGE. Who *were* you then.

MARLEY. In life I was your partner, Jacob Marley.

SCROOGE. Can you - can you sit down?

MARLEY. I can.

SCROOGE. Do it then.

(The ghost sits as if he were quite used to it.)

MARLEY. You don't believe in me.

SCROOGE. I don't.

MARLEY. What evidence would you have of my reality, beyond that of your senses?

SCROOGE. I don't know.

MARLEY. Why do you doubt your senses?

SCROOGE. Because a little thing affects them. You may be an undigested bit of beef, a crumb of cheese. There's more of gravy than of grave about you. Humbug, I tell you - humbug!

(At this the Spirit raises a fearful cry, shakes its chain; Scrooge almost swoons. Then he sees with horror the phantom taking off its kerchief from its head, and the lower jaw drops to its breast. Scrooge falls to his knees and clasps his hands before his face.)

SCROOGE. Mercy! Dreadful apparition, why do you trouble me?

MARLEY. Man of the worldly mind! Do you believe in me or not?

SCROOGE. I do. I must. But why do spirits walk the earth, and why do they come to me?

MARLEY. It is required of every man, that the spirit within him should walk abroad among his fellowmen; and if that spirit goes not forth in life, it is condemned to do so after death. It is doomed to wander through the world - oh, woe is me! - and witness what it cannot share, but might have shared on earth, and turned to happiness! *(Again it cries, shakes its chains, and wrings its hands.)*

SCROOGE. *(trembling)* You are fettered. Tell me why.

MARLEY. I wear the chain I forged in life. I made it link by link, and yard by yard; I girded it on of my own free will, and of my own free will I wore it. Is its pattern strange to you?

SCROOGE. *(looking behind himself)* Jacob *(imploringly)*, Old Jacob Marley, tell me more. Speak comfort to me. Jacob.

MARLEY. I have none to give. It comes from other regions, Ebenezer Scrooge, and is conveyed by other ministers to other kinds of men. I cannot rest, I cannot stay, I cannot linger anywhere.

SCROOGE. You travel fast?

MARLEY. On the wings of the wind.

SCROOGE. You must have got over a great quantity of ground in seven years.

(The ghost sets up another cry and shakes its chains.)

MARLEY. Oh! Captive bound and double-ironed, not to know this earth must pass *(SLIDE No. 2A: Chains on bed curtain.)* into eternity before the good of which it is susceptible is all developed. Not to know any Christian spirit will find its mortal life too short for its task. Yet such was I! Oh! Such was I! *(Wash projection out with dark color till cue for slide No. 2)*

SCROOGE. But you were always a good man of business, Jacob.

MARLEY. Business! *(wringing its hands)* Mankind was my business. The common welfare was my business. The dealings of my trade were but a drop of water in the ocean of my business. *(Holds up its chain and flings it down again)* At this time of the rolling year I suffer most. Why did I walk through crowds of fellow-beings with my eyes turned down, and never raise them to that blessed Star which led the Wise Men to a poor abode? *(Scrooge begins to quake exceedingly)* Hear me! My time is nearly gone.

SCROOGE. I will. But don't be hard upon me!

MARLEY. I am here to warn you that you have yet a chance and hope of escaping my fate. A chance and hope of my procuring, Ebenezer.

SCROOGE. You were always a good friend to me. Thank'ee!

MARLEY. You will be haunted by three spirits.

SCROOGE. *(faltering)* Is that the chance and hope you mentioned, Jacob?

MARLEY. It is.

SCROOGE. I - I think I'd rather not.

MARLEY. Without their visits you cannot hope to shun the path I tread. Expect the first tomorrow, when the bell tolls one.

SCROOGE. Couldn't I take 'em all at once, and have it over?

MARLEY. Expect the second on the next night at the same hour. The third upon the next night at the stroke of midnight. Look to see me no more. *(It winds the kerchief around its head. The sound of the teeth is heard when the jaws are brought together. It goes to the window and beckons Scrooge. When he is within two paces Marley raises his hand. The sound of noises are heard: wailing, lamentations of regret, sorrow, and self-accusation. Marley's ghost joins in the wails and floats out the window. Scrooge's curiosity takes him to the window. Enter spirits.)*

SPIRITS. *(CHAIN SLIDE No. 2B appears.)* The air was filled with phantoms, / wandering hither and thither in restless haste / and moaning as they went. / Every one of them wore chains like Marley's Ghost; / Some few (they might be guilty governments) were linked together; / none were free.

SCROOGE. Scrooge had been quite familiar with one old ghost, with a monstrous iron safe attached to its ankle,

SPIRIT. who cried piteously at being unable to assist a wretched woman with an infant.

MARLEY. He had lost the power for good, for ever...

(Lights go to dark. All ghosts and Marley exeunt.)

SCROOGE. And being worn out from the emotions, Scrooge fell asleep upon the instant.

STAVE TWO: CHRISTMAS PAST
The First of the Three Spirits

(Stave II sign is brought on. In the darkness the bell tolls.)

SCROOGE. Quarter past; half past; The hour itself and nothing else!

> *(The bell tolls ONE. Again lights flash up, and the curtain of his bed are drawn.)*

SCROOGE. The curtains of his bed, were drawn aside, I tell you, by a hand.

SLIDE No. 3, a hand, up briefly.

(Scrooge is face to face with "the unearthly visitor who drew them, as close to it as I am to you, and I am standing in spirit at your elbow.") It was a strange figure -

SPIRIT. like a child:

SCROOGE. yet not so like a child

SPIRIT. as like an old man.

SCROOGE. It's hair was white as if with age

(Spirit turns its back to audience)

SPIRIT. *(turning back)* and yet the face had not a wrinkle in it, and the tenderest bloom was on the skin.

SCROOGE. From the crown of its head there sprung a bright clear jet of light; it carried a great extinguisher for a cap *(which it holds under its arm and uses, cap on, cap off)*

SPIRIT. What was light one instant, at another time was dark, now a thing with one arm, now with one leg, now with twenty legs, now a pair of legs without a head, now a head without a body. *(demonstrates all this)*

SCROOGE. Are you the spirit, sir, whose coming was foretold to me?

SPIRIT. I am!

SCROOGE. Who, and what are you?

SPIRIT. I am the Ghost of Christmas Past.

SCROOGE. Long Past?

PAST. No. Your Past.

SCROOGE. Scrooge had a special desire to see the Spirit in his cap. *(gestures and begs)*

PAST. What! Would you so soon put out, with worldly hands, the light I give? Is it not enough that you are one of those whose passions made this cap, and force me to wear it low upon my brow!

SCROOGE. What business brought you here?

PAST. Your welfare.

SCROOGE. A night of sleep would be conducive to that end.

PAST. Your reclamation then. Take heed! *(puts out its hand and clasps him gently by the arm)* Rise! and walk with me!

SCROOGE. I am mortal, and liable to fall.

PAST. Bear but a touch of my hand *there*, *(on his heart)* and you shall be upheld in more than this! *(Bed and curtains are removed).*

SCROOGE. They passed through the wall, *(Traveller opens.)*

(SLIDE No. 4, Open road.) and stood upon an open road, with fields on either hand. The city had entirely vanished!

PAST. The darkness and the mist had vanished with it, for it was a clear, cold, winter day, with snow upon the ground.

SCROOGE. *(clasping his hands together)* I was bred in this place! I was a boy here! *(The Spirit gazes at him mildly. Scrooge still feels its gentle touch.)* He was conscious of a thousand odors floating in the air, a thousand hopes, and joys, and cares long, long forgotten!

PAST. Your lip is trembling. And what is that upon your cheek?

SCROOGE. *(hiding the tear)* Scrooge begged the Ghost to lead him where he would. *(They set off.)*

PAST. You recollect the way?

SCROOGE. *(with fervor)* Remember it! I could walk it blindfold.

PAST. Strange to have forgotten it for so many years! Let us go in.

SCROOGE. Scrooge recognized every gate, and post, and tree; until a little market town appeared with its bridge, its church, and winding river. *(Children on shaggy ponies call and sing to one another.)*

PAST. These are but shadows of the things that have been. They have no consciousness of us.

(Snow falls, Townspeople enter singing 'Joy to the World'.)

SCROOGE. *(as children and other jocund travelers come on)* Scrooge knew and named them every one. Why did his cold eye glisten, and his heart leap up as they went past! Why was he filled with gladness when he heard them give each other Merry Christmas, as they parted for their several homes! What was Merry Christmas to Scrooge? Out upon Merry Christmas! *(SLIDE out.)*

PAST. The school is not quite deserted. A solitary child, neglected by his friends, is left there still.

SCROOGE. Scrooge said he knew it. And he sobbed. *(They enter)*

SLIDE No. 5, SCHOOLROOM.

BOY. In a long, bare, melancholy room a lonely boy is reading near a feeble fire.

SCROOGE. *(Scrooge weeps to see his poor forgotten self as he used to be.)* Suddenly a man in foreign garments appears leading an ass. *(ecstatic)* Why it's Ali Baba! It's dear old honest Ali Baba! Yes, yes, I know! One Christmas time, when yonder solitary child was left here all alone, he *did* come, for the first time, just like that. Poor boy! And the Three Musketeers! *(they enter swords out and cross to exit)*

THREE MUSKETEERS. *(shouting)* All for one! And one for all!

SCROOGE. *(after drying his eyes with his cuff)* I wish, but it's too late now.

PAST. What is the matter?

SCROOGE. Nothing. Nothing. There was a boy singing a Christmas Carol at my door last night. I should like to have given him something: that's all.

PAST. *(smiling thoughtfully, waving his hand)* Let us see another Christmas!

SCROOGE. Scrooge's former self grew larger at the words, and the room became a little darker and more dirty; but how this all was brought about, Scrooge knew no more than you do. There he was, alone again, when all the other children had gone home for the jolly holidays. *(He is not reading, but walking up and down in despair. Scrooge shakes his head*

*mournfully and glances at the door. It opens and a little
girl darts in and puts her arms about his neck, often kissing him.)*

GIRL. Dear, dear brother. I have come to bring you
home, dear brother! *(clapping her hands and bending
down to laugh)* To bring you home, home, home!

YOUNG SCROOGE. Home, little Fan?

GIRL. *(with glee)* Yes! Home for good and all. Home,
for ever and ever. Father is so much kinder than he
used to be, that home's like Heaven! He spoke so
gently to me one dear night when I was going to
bed, that I was not afraid to ask him once more if
you might come home; and he said, Yes, you
should; and sent me in a coach to bring you. *(sound
of horses outside)* And you're to be a man! And are
never to come back here.

YOUNG SCROOGE. You are quite a woman, little Fan.
*(She claps her hands and laughs, and tries to touch his
head; but being too little, laughs again, and stands on
tiptoe to embrace him. Then she drags him towards the
door, and he follows.)*

SCHOOLMASTER. *(in a terrible voice)* Bring down
Master Scrooge's box, there! *(appears and shakes
hands and glares at young Scrooge with ferocious conde-
scension.)* He then produced a decanter

YOUNG SCROOGE. of curiously light wine,

SCHOOLMASTER. and a block

FAN. of curiously heavy cake *(Schoolmaster serves them)*

SERVANT. at the same time sending out a meager servant to offer a glass of 'something' to the post boy,

POST BOY. who answered that he thanked the gentleman, but if it was the same tap as he had tasted before, he had rather not.

DRIVER. *(enters)* Master Scrooge's trunk being by this time tied on to the top of the chaise, *(a bench is brought to seat them as the space trunk is tied on)*

YOUNG SCROOGE. the children bade the schoolmaster goodbye right willingly;

FAN. and getting into it, drove gaily down the garden sweep;

(Both are aboard the chaise, with driver and footman, the whip is cracked and off they go.)

YOUNG SCROOGE. the quick wheels dashing the hoarfrost and snow

FAN. like spray! *(exeunt from stage left removing bench. SLIDE out.)*

PAST. Always a delicate creature, whom a breath might have withered. But she had a large heart!

SCROOGE. So she had. You're right. I'll not deny it, Spirit. God forbid!

PAST. She died a woman, and had, as I think, children.

SCROOGE. One child.

PAST. True. Your nephew!

SCROOGE. *(uneasy in mind)* Yes. Suddenly they were in a city.

PAST. *(stopping at a certain door)* Do you know this place?

SCROOGE. Know it! Was I apprenticed here? *(they enter to find an old gentleman in a Welch wig)* Why, it's old Fezziwig! Bless his heart; it's Fezziwig alive again!

SLIDE No. 6, FEZZIWIG' S WAREHOUSE

FEZZIWIG. *(Fezziwig lays down his pen, looks up at the clock (seven), rubs his hands, adjusts his capacious waistcoat; laughs all over himself, from his shoes to his organ of benevolence; calls out in a comfortable, oily, rich, fat, jovial voice:)* Yo ho, there! Ebenezar! Dick! Hang the party decorations!

(Enter the young Scrooge and his fellow apprentice with real decorations evergreens to hang on wire, center, connected by red ribbons criss -crossing the stage to four beribboned poles, are to be set into pre-positioned stands, and are brought on by Fezziwig workers and other players.)

SCROOGE. *(to Ghost)* Dick Wilkins, to be sure! Bless me, yes. There he is. He was very much attached to me, was Dick. Poor Dick! Dear, dear!

FEZZIWIG. Yo ho, my boys. No more work tonight. Christmas Eve, Dick. Christmas, Ebenezer! Let's have the shutters up *(a sharp clap of his hands)* before a man can say, Jack Robinson!

SCROOGE. You wouldn't believe how those two fellows went at it!

EBENEZER. They charged into the street with the shutters *(opening and closing space doors to the street, downstage.)* - one

DICK. two,

EBENEZER. three -

DICK. had 'em up in their places - *(on the space wall near the audience)*

EBENEZER. four,

DICK. five,

EBENEZER. six - barred 'em and pinned 'em -

DICK. seven,

EBENEZER. eight,

DICK. nine - and came back before you could have got to twelve, *(opening and closing space doors)*

EBENEZER. panting like race horses.

FEZZIWIG. Hilli-ho! Clear away, my lads, and let's have lots of room here! Hilli-ho, Dick! Chirrup, Ebenezer!

DICK. Clear away!

EBENEZER. There was nothing they wouldn't have cleared away,

DICK. or couldn't have cleared away, with old Fezziwig looking on.

EBENEZER. It was done in a minute.

DICK. Every movable was packed off, as if it were dismissed from public life for evermore;

EBENEZER. the floor was swept and watered,

DICK. the lamps trimmed,

EBENEZER. fuel was heaped upon the fire; *(Broom, lamps, firewood are all space objects)*

DICK. and the warehouse was as snug, and warm and dry,

EBENEZER. and bright a ball-room, as you would desire to see

DICK. upon a winter's night.

FIDDLER. In came a fiddler with a music-book, and tuned like fifty stomach-aches.

MRS. FEZZIWIG. In came Mrs. Fezziwig, one vast substantial smile.

MISSES FEZZIWIGS. In came the Miss Fezziwigs, beaming and lovable.

YOUTH. In came the young followers, whose hearts they broke.

MAID. In came the housemaid with her cousin,

BAKER. the baker.

COOK. In came the cook,

MILKMAN. with her brother's particular friend,

COOK. the milkman.

BOY. In came the boy from over the way,

MRS. FEZZIWIG. who was suspected of not having board enough from his master;

BOY. trying to hide himself behind the girl from next door but one,

GIRL. who was proved to have had her ears pulled by her Mistress.

- In they all came,
- one after another,
- some shyly,
- some boldly,
- some gracefully,
- some awkwardly,
- some pushing,
- some pulling,
- in they all came, anyhow and everyhow.

(Music for Square Dance)

- Away they all went, hands half round,
- and back again the other way;
- down the middle,
- and up again,
- round and round
- in various stages of affectionate grouping;
- old couple always turning up in the wrong place;

  - new couple starting off again as soon as they
got there,
  - all top couples at last and not a bottom one to
help them.

FEZZIWIG. *(clapping hands to stop dance)* Well done! *(all clap)*

FIDDLER. And the fiddler plunged his hot face into a pot of porter,

DICK. especially provided for that purpose.

FIDDLER. He instantly began again, as if the other fiddler had been carried home exhausted; and he were a brand-new man resolved to beat him out of sight.

  - There were more dances,
  - and there were forfeits,
  - and more dances,
  - and there was cake,
  - and there was mulled wine,
  - and there was a great piece of Cold Roast,
  - and there was a great piece of Cold Boiled,
  - and there were mince pies,
  - and plenty of beer.

FIDDLER. But the great effect of the evening came when the fiddler (an artful dog, mind!) struck up 'Sir Roger de Coverly'!

FEZZIWIG. Then old Fezziwig stood out to dance, with Mrs. Fezziwig.

MRS. FEZZIWIG. Top couple, too; with a good stiff piece of work cut out for them;

- people who were not to be trifled with;
- people who *would* dance, and had no notion of walking.
- Bow and curtsy; and retreat,
- corkscrew; thread the needle.

FEZZIWIG. Fezziwig cut so deftly, that he appeared to wink with his legs, and came upon his feet again without a stagger.

FIDDLER. When the clock struck eleven, this domestic ball broke up.

FEZZIWIG. Mr. and Mrs. Fezziwig took their stations,

MRS. FEZZIWIG. one on either side the door, *(door is in space, downstage cnter.)*

FEZZIWIG. and shaking hands individually with every person as he or she went out,

MRS. FEZZIWIG. wished him or her a Merry Christmas. *(The apprentices take down the decorations, helped by Fezziwig and his family.)*

PAST. A small matter, to make these silly folks so full of gratitude.

SCROOGE. Small!

PAST. Why! Is it not? He has spent but a few pounds of your mortal money: three or four, perhaps. Is that so much that he deserves this praise?

SCROOGE. *(heated by the remark)* It isn't that, Spirit.

(Beribboned pole are removed and traveller closes; SLIDE No. 5 out.)

He has the power to render us happy or unhappy, to make our service light or burdensome; a pleasure or a toil. The happiness he gives, is quite as great as if it cost a fortune. *(Remembers)*

PAST. What is the matter?

SCROOGE. Nothing particular.

PAST. Something, I think.

SCROOGE. No. I should like to be able to say a word or two to my clerk just now! That's all.

(SLIDE OUT. Ebenezer and Dick turn down the lights as Scrooge and Spirit go through a wall into the open air.)

PAST. My time grows short. Quick!

(A young woman appears in a mourning dress.)

BELLE. It matters little, to you, very little. Another idol has displaced me, and if it can cheer and comfort you in time to come, as I would have tried to do, I have no just cause to grieve.

SCROOGE. *(made-up and costumed as he has been)* What idol has displaced you?

BELLE. A golden one.

SCROOGE. There is nothing on which the world is so hard as poverty.

BELLE. You fear the world too much. I have seen your nobler aspirations fall off one by one, until the master-passion, GAIN, engrosses you. Have I not?

SCROOGE. What then? Even if I have grown so much wiser, what then? I am not changed towards you. *(She shakes her head.)* Am I?

BELLE. Our contract is an old one. When it was made, you were another man.

SCROOGE. *(impatiently)* I was a boy.

BELLE. You were not what you are. I am. How often and how keenly I have thought of this, I will not say. It is enough that I *have* thought of it, and can release you.

SCROOGE. Have I ever sought release?

BELLE. In words. No, never.

SCROOGE. In what then?

BELLE. In an altered spirit; in another atmosphere of life. In everything that made my love of any worth or value in your sight. Tell me, would you seek me out and try to win me now? Ah, no!

SCROOGE. *(knowing she is right)* You think not.

BELLE. If you were free today, can I believe that you would choose a dowerless girl - you who weigh everything by Gain? I release you. With a full heart, for the love of him you once were. *(turns her head away)* You may - I half hope you will - have pain in this. A very, very brief time, and you will dismiss the recollection of it, gladly, as an unprofitable dream, from which you awoke. May you be happy in the life you have chosen. *(She leaves him, "and they parted.")*

SCROOGE. Spirit! Show me no more! Conduct me home. Why do you delight to torture me?

PAST. One shadow more! To see her children and whom she married, and how they celebrate Christmas.

SCROOGE. No more! I don't wish to see it. No more!

PAST. These are shadows of the things that have been. They are what they are.

SCROOGE. Remove me! I cannot bear it! Haunt me no longer! *(Wrestles with the Spirit; seizes the extinguisher cap of the Spirit and presses it down on its head. The Spirit drops so that the extinguisher covers its whole form. But the light streams out from under it. Scrooge is exhausted and falls on his own bed and is in a heavy sleep.)*

INTERMISSION

ACT II

STAVE THREE: *Christmas Present*
The Second of the Great Spirits

(STAVE III sign is brought on. A clock tower bell tolls ONE. Scrooge wakes in the middle of a snore.)

SCROOGE. No shape appeared *(he trembles violently)*; five minutes, ten minutes, a quarter of an hour went by, yet nothing came. *(a blaze of ruddy light touches his bed, he senses the source of the light to be in the next room. Gets up and shuffles in his slippers to the door.)*

VOICE. Enter, Ebenezer Scrooge! *(Traveller opens for SLIDE NO. 7: ABUNDANCE. The space transforms, slide shows walls hung with living green, with holly and mistletoe and mirrors of light. A blaze in the fireplace. A jolly giant carries a torch, like Plenty's horn.)*

GHOST. Come in! Come in! And know me better, man! I am the Ghost of Christmas Present. Look upon me! You have never seen the like of me before!

SCROOGE. Never. Spirit, conduct me where you will. I went forth last night on compulsion, and I learnt a lesson which is working now.

PRESENT. Touch my robe! *(As Scrooge does so the room, the ruddy glow, the hour of night vanishes. SLIDE No. 7 out . SLIDE No. 8 up: LONDON CHRISTMAS.Cratchit house of burlap scrim appears on wire, pulled on by a player.)*

SCROOGE. They stood in the city streets on Christmas morning. *(snow falls)*

CHORUS. The people made a rough, but brisk and not unpleasant kind of music
    - in scraping the snow from the pavement in front of their dwellings,
    - and from the tops of their houses,

CHILD. whence it was a mad delight to the children to see it come plumping down into the road below,

CHILD. and splitting into artificial little snow-storms.
    - The people shoveling away were jovial and full of glee;
    - calling out to one another from the parapets,
    - and now and then exchanging a facetious snowball -
    - laughing heartily if it went right,
    - and not less heartily if it went wrong.

POULTERER. *(carrying squawking space chickens)* The poulterers' shops were still half open,

FRUITERER. and the fruiterers were radiant in their glory and winking in wanton slyness at the girls as they went by,

GIRL. glancing demurely at the hung-up mistletoe.

OTHERS. There were pears and apples, clustered high
in blooming pyramids;

  - there were piles of filberts, mossy and brown,
  -   recalling, in their fragrance, ancient walks
among the woods,
  - and pleasant shufflings ankle deep through
withered leaves.
  (Church bells)
  - But soon the steeples called good people all,
to church and chapel
  (Entering)-   and away they came, flocking
through the streets in their best clothes,
  - and with their gayest faces.
  - At the same time there emerged from scores
of bye streets, lanes,
  - and nameless turnings, innumerable poor
people, carrying their dinners to the baker's shops
to be cooked.

*(Present takes his torch and sprinkles incense on their
food; lifting a cover or two as needed.)*

PRESENT. And it was a very uncommon kind of torch
he waved,

SCROOGE. for once or twice when there were angry
words between some dinner-carriers *(who have jos-
tled each other)*,

PRESENT. he shed a few drops of water on them,

SCROOGE. and their good humor was restored directly.

CARRIERS. For, they said, It was a shame to quarrel upon Christmas Day.
- And so it was!
- God love it, so it was!

SCROOGE. Is there a peculiar flavor in what you sprinkle from your torch?

PRESENT. There is. My own.

SCROOGE. Would it apply to any kind of dinner on this day?

PRESENT. To any kindly given. To a poor one most.

SCROOGE. Why to a poor one most?

PRESENT. Because it needs it most. And with that, he went straight to Bob Cratchit's dwelling,

SCROOGE. Scrooge holding to his robe,

PRESENT. and on the threshold of the door blessed it with his torch

SCROOGE. Think of that! Bob had but fifteen 'Bob' a-week himself; and yet the Ghost of Christmas Present blessed his four-roomed house!

MRS. CRATCHIT. Then up rose Mrs. Cratchit, Cratchit's wife, dressed out but poorly in a twice-turned gown, but brave in ribbons, which are cheap and make a goodly show for sixpence; and she laid the cloth,

BELINDA. assisted by Belinda Cratchit, second of her daughters, also brave in ribbons;

PETER. while Master Peter Cratchit plunged a fork into the saucepan of potatoes *(space objects, from fork to stove)*, and getting the corners of his monstrous shirt-collar,

BELINDA. Bob's private property,

PETER. into his mouth, rejoiced to find himself so gallantly attired,

BELINDA. and yearned to show his linen in the fashionable parks.

BOY. And now the two smaller Cratchits, boy

GIRL. and girl,

BOY. came tearing in,

GIRL. screaming that outside the baker's they had smelled the goose,

BOY. and known it for their own;

GIRL. and basking in luxurious thoughts of sage and onion,

BOY. these young Cratchits danced about the table,

GIRL. and exalted Master Peter Cratchit to the skies,

PETER. while he, not proud, although his collars nearly choked him, blew the fire,

BOY. until the slow potatoes bubbling up, knocked loudly at the saucepan lid,

GIRL. to be let out and peeled.

MRS. CRATCHIT. What has ever got your precious father then. And your brother, Tiny Tim; and

Martha warn't as late last Christmas Day by half-an-hour.

MARTHA. *(entering)* Here's Martha, mother.

BOY. Here's Martha, mother! Hurrah!

GIRL. There's *such* a goose, Martha!

MRS. CRATCHIT. *(kissing her a dozen times, and taking off her shawl and bonnet with officious zeal)* Why, bless your heart alive, my dear, how late you are!

MARTHA. We'd a deal of work to finish up last night, and had to clear away this morning, mother!

MRS. CRATCHIT. Well! Never mind so long as you are come. Sit ye down before the fire, my dear, and have a warm, Lord bless ye! *(Two six foot benches can handle the family, moving them from fire to table and back, as needed.)*

GIRL. No! There's Father coming.

BOY. Hide, Martha, hide.

MARTHA. So Martha hid herself,

CRATCHIT. and in came little Bob, the father, his thread-bare clothes darned up and brushed, to look seasonable,

TINY TIM. and Tiny Tim upon his shoulder.

CRATCHIT. Alas, for Tiny Tim. *(letting him down for Boy and Girl to take him to a seat near the hearth)*

BOY. He bore a little crutch,

GIRL. and had his limbs supported by an iron frame!

CRATCHIT. Why, where's our Martha?

MRS. CRATCHIT. Not coming.

CRATCHIT. *(declension of high spirits)* Not coming! Not coming upon Christmas Day!

MARTHA. Martha didn't like to see him disappointed,

CRATCHIT. and ran into his arms,

BOY AND GIRL. while the two young Cratchits hustled Tiny Tim,

BELINDA. and bore him off into the wash-house

TINY TIM. that he might hear the pudding singing in the copper.

MRS. CRATCHIT. And how did little Tim behave?

CRATCHIT. As good as gold, and better. Somehow he gets thoughtful sitting by himself so much, and thinks the strangest things you ever heard. He told me, coming home, that he hoped the people saw him in church, because he was a cripple, and it might be pleasant to them to remember upon Christmas Day, who made the lame walk and blind men see.

MRS. CRATCHIT. His active little crutch was heard upon the floor,

TINY TIM. and back came Tiny Tim,

BOY. escorted by his brother

GIRL. and sister

BOY. to his stool,

GIRL. before the fire;

CRATCHIT. and while Bob, turning up his cuffs -

MRS. CRATCHIT. as if, poor fellow, they were capable of being made more shabby -

CRATCHIT. compounded some hot mixture in a jug with gin and lemons *(stirs it round and round and puts it on the hob to simmer)*;

PETER. Master Peter

BOY AND GIRL. and the two ubiquitous young Cratchits

PETER. went to fetch the goose,

BOY AND GIRL. with which they soon returned in high procession.

BELINDA. Such a bustle ensued that you might have thought a goose the rarest of all birds:

CRATCHIT. a feathered phenomenon,

MARTHA. to which a black swan was a matter of course;

BELINDA. and in truth it was something very like it in that house.

MRS. CRATCHIT. Mrs. Cratchit made the gravy hissing hot.

PETER. Master Peter mashed the potatoes with incredible vigor.

BELINDA. Miss Belinda sweetened up the apple sauce;

MARTHA. Martha dusted the hot plates;

CRATCHIT. Bob took Tiny Tim beside him in a tiny corner at the table

BOY AND GIRL. the two young Cratchits set silverware for everybody,

BELINDA. not forgetting themselves,

BOY. and crammed spoons into their mouths,

GIRL. lest they should shriek before their turn came to be helped.

MARTHA. At last the dishes were set on, and grace was said.

BELINDA. It was succeeded by a breathless pause,

MRS. CRATCHIT. *(looking slowly along the knife) as* Mrs. Cratchit prepared to plunge the knife in the breast. *(She does.)*

(A murmur of delight from all. Tiny Tim beats on the table with his knife.)

TINY TIM. Hurrah!

(The meal is eaten within the next seven or eight lines.)

CRATCHIT. There never was such a goose.

PETER. It's tenderness

MARTHA. and flavor,

BELINDA. size

MRS. CRATCHIT. and cheapness,

CRATCHIT. were the themes of universal admiration.

MRS. CRATCHIT. Indeed, as Mrs. Cratchit said with great delight

BELINDA. surveying one small atom of a bone upon the dish

MRS. CRATCHIT. they hadn't ate it all at last!

PETER. Yet everyone had had enough,

BOY. and the youngest Cratchits in particular

GIRL. were steeped in sage and onions to the eyebrows!

BELINDA. But now, the plates being changed by Miss Belinda,

MRS. CRATCHIT. Mrs. Cratchit left the room alone -

MARTHA. too nervous to bear witnesses -

CRATCHIT. to take the pudding up, and bring it in.

GIRL. Suppose it should not be done enough!

BELINDA. Suppose it should break in turning out!

BOY. Suppose somebody should have got over the wall of the backyard and stolen it.

CRATCHIT. All sorts of horrors were supposed.

MRS. CRATCHIT. Hallo!

PETER. A great deal of steam!

MRS. CRATCHIT. (off) The pudding Is out of the copper.

PETER. A smell like washing day!

MARTHA. That was the cloth.

BELINDA. A smell like an eating house and a pastry cook's.

CRATCHIT. That was the pudding.

MRS. CRATCHIT. In half a minute Mrs. Cratchit entered: flushed, but smiling proudly: with the pudding,

BOY. like a speckled cannon ball,

GIRL. so hard and firm,

PETER. *(lighting the flame)* blazing in half of half-a-quartern of ignited brandy,

TINY TIM. with Christmas holly stuck into the top.

CRATCHIT. Oh, a wonderful pudding! He regarded it as the greatest success achieved by Mrs. Cratchit since their marriage.

MRS. CRATCHIT. Now that the weight was off her mind, she confessed she had her doubts about the quantity of flour.

GIRL. Everybody had something to say about it,

BELINDA. but nobody said or thought it was at all a small pudding for a large family.

CRATCHIT. It would have been flat heresy to do so.

PETER. Any Cratchit would have blushed to hint at such a thing.

BOY. At last the dinner was all done,

BELINDA. the cloth was cleared,

MARTHA. the hearth swept,

CRATCHIT. and the fire made up.

PETER. The compound in the jug being tasted, and considered perfect,

GIRL. apples and oranges were put upon the table,

BOY. and a shovel-full of chestnuts on the fire.

CRATCHIT. Then all the Cratchit family drew round the hearth,

MRS. CRATCHIT. in what Bob Cratchit called a circle,

MARTHA. meaning half a one;

CRATCHIT. and brought out the family display of glass;

BELINDA. two tumblers, and a custard-cup without a handle.

MRS. CRATCHIT. These held the hot stuff from the jug, however, as well as golden goblets would have done;

CRATCHIT. A Merry Christmas to us all, my dears. God bless us!

ALL. God bless us!

TINY TIM. God bless us every one!

(Bob takes Tiny Tim's withered hand and puts him by his side, as if he dreads Tim will be taken from him.)

SCROOGE. Spirit, tell me if Tiny Tim will live.

PRESENT. I see a vacant seat in the poor chimney corner, and a crutch without an owner, carefully preserved. If these shadows remain unaltered by the future, the child will die.

SCROOGE. No, no, oh no, kind Spirit! Say he will be spared.

PRESENT. What then? If he be like to die, he had better do it, and decrease the surplus population.

(Scrooge hangs his head in penitence and grief.)

MRS. CRATCHIT. All this time the chestnuts and the jug went round and round,

MARTHA. and bye and bye they had a song from Tiny Tim.

(Dickens did not write the words for this song, but perhaps Yeats did in The Stolen Child, whose refrain runs: 'Come away, O human child! To the waters and the wild - With a faery, hand in hand, For the world is more full of weeping than you can understand.')

PRESENT. There was nothing of high mark in this. They were not a handsome family, they were not well dressed;

MARTHA. their shoes were far from being water-proof;

BELINDA. their clothes were scanty;

PETER. and Peter might have known,

BELINDA. and very likely did -

PETER. the inside of a pawnbroker's,

MRS. CRATCHIT. but they were happy,

BOY. grateful,

MARTHA. pleased with one another,

GIRL. and contented with the time. *(The family rise, remove the benches, exeunt.)*

PRESENT. And when they faded in the bright sprinklings of the Spirit's torch at parting,

SCROOGE. Scrooge had his eye upon them, and especially on Tiny Tim, until the last. *(LONDON CHRISTMAS SLIDE No. 8 out and house scrim off at exit.)*

PRESENT. And now without a word of warning from the Ghost, they stood upon a bleak and desert moor,

SCROOGE. where monstrous masses of rude stone were cast about, as though it were the burial place of giants.

PRESENT. Down in the west the setting sun had left a streak of fiery red, which glared upon the desolation like a sullen eye.

SCROOGE. What place is this?

PRESENT. A place where Miners live, who labor in the bowels of the earth. But they know me. See!

(A cheerful company assembles round an old, old man and woman. He is singing them a Christmas song, 'Deck the Halls With Boughs of Holly'; all join in the chorus and dance. The howling wind competes with them. When they raise their voices, the old couple sing blithe and loud. Exeunt omnes.)

PRESENT. Hold my robe! (They sail aloft.)

SCROOGE. Whereto? Not to sea?

PRESENT. *(A thundering of water, much to Scrooge's horror.)* To sea.

SCROOGE. Some league or two from shore, there stood a solitary lighthouse, and storm birds

(SLIDE No. 9, LIGHTHOUSE)

PRESENT. born of the wind one might suppose, rose and fell like the waves they skimmed!

LIGHTHOUSE KEEPER. But even here two men had lit the fire

HIS PARTNER. that shed out a ray of brightness on the awful sea.

(The two men join hands and wish each other Merry Christmas, as they exeunt.)

PRESENT. Again the Ghost sped on, above the black and heaving sea - on, on, -

SCROOGE. until, being far away from any shore, they lighted on a ship,

PRESENT. by the helmsman at the wheel, the officers who had the watch;

SCROOGE. the lookout in the bow; dark, ghostly figures in their several stations.

PRESENT. But every man among them hummed a Christmas tune, or had a Christmas thought,

SAILOR ONE. or spoke below his breath to his companion of some bygone Christmas Day,

SAILOR TWO. with homeward hopes belonging to it.

SAILOR ONE. And every man on board, good or bad, had a kinder word for another on that day,

SAILOR TWO. and had remembered those he cared for at a distance,

SAILOR ONE. and had known that they delighted to remember him.

SCROOGE. It was a great surprise to Scrooge, while listening to the moaning of the wind, to hear a hearty laugh.

(SLIDE No. 9 out; traveller closes and players entering bring on white curtain.)

It was a much greater surprise to recognize it as his own nephew's, and to find himself in a bright, dry, gleaming room,

PRESENT. with the Spirit standing smiling by his side.

FRED. Ha, ha! Ha, ha, ha!

(Fred's wife and friends all laugh as lustily.)

FRED. He said that Christmas was a humbug, as I live. He believed it too!

WIFE. More shame for him, Fred!

PRESENT. Bless those women: they never do anything by halves. They're always in earnest.

FRED. He's a comical old fellow, that's the truth: and not so pleasant as he might be. However, his offenses carry their own punishment.

WIFE. I have no patience with him.*(Her sisters and the others express the same opinion. All pour tea and eat cake.)*

FRED. I am sorry for him; I couldn't be angry with him if I tried. Who suffers by his ill whims! Himself, always. Here, he takes it into his head to dislike us, and he won't come to dine with us. What's the consequence? He don't lose much of a dinner.

WIFE. Indeed, I think he loses a very good dinner. *(The others agree with her, and must be allowed to be competent judges for they have just finished dinner, and are at dessert, clustered around the fire, by lamplight.)*

FRED. Well! I'm very glad to hear it, because I haven't great faith in these young housekeepers. What do *you* say, Topper?

TOPPER. Topper had clearly got his eyes upon one of Scrooge's niece's sisters, for he answered that a bachelor was a wretched outcast, who had no right to express an opinion on the subject.

PLUMP GIRL. Whereas Scrooge's niece's sister - the plump one with the lace tucker; not the one with the roses - blushed.

WIFE. Do go on, Fred. *(clapping her hands)* He never finishes what he begins to say! He is such a ridiculous fellow.

FRED. *(revels in a laugh, which everyone follows though the plump girl tries to stop it with aromatic vinegar)* I was going to say that the consequence of his not making merry with us is that he loses some pleasant moments, which could do him no harm. I am sure he loses pleasanter companions than he can find in his own thoughts.

WIFE. After tea they had some music.

FRIENDS. And knew what they were about when they sung a Glee or a Catch, I can assure you.

PLUMP GIRL. For they were a musical family,

TOPPER. especially Topper, who could growl away in the bass and never get red in the face.

WIFE. Scrooge's niece played well upon the harp *(plays)*;

FRIEND. and played among other tunes a simple little air,

WIFE. a mere nothing: you might learn to whistle it in two minutes.

SCROOGE. *(listening)* Scrooge softened more and more, and thought that if he could have listened to it often, years ago, he might have cultivated the kindnesses of life.

PRESENT. But they didn't devote the whole evening to music.

FRIEND. After a while they played at forfeits!

FRED. For it is good to be children sometimes,

PRESENT. and never better than at Christmas, when its mighty Founder was a child himself.

WIFE. Stop! There was first a game at blind-man's buff.

FRIEND. Of course there was. *(They start)*

SCROOGE. The way he went after that plump sister in the lace tucker, was an outrage on the credulity of human nature.

TOPPER. Knocking down the fireirons, tumbling over the chairs,

PLUMP GIRL. wherever she went there went he,

TOPPER. bumping against the piano, smothering himself among the curtains.

SCROOGE. He always knew where the plump sister was.

PRESENT. He wouldn't catch anybody else.

(Others fall against him, get in his way, he makes a feint of endeavoring to catch them, and sidles off toward the plump girl.)

PLUMP GIRL. She often cried out that it wasn't fair.

SCROOGE. And it really was not.

TOPPER. But when at last, he caught her;

PLUMP GIRL. when, in spite of all her silken rustling, and her rapid flutterings past him,

TOPPER. he got her into a corner whence there was no escape;

PLUMP GIRL. then his conduct was the most execrable.

TOPPER. For his pretending not to know her;

PLUMP GIRL. his pretending it was necessary to touch her headdress,

TOPPER. and a certain chain about her neck;

PLUMP GIRL. was vile, monstrous!

SCROOGE. No doubt she told him her opinion of it, when, another blind-man being in office,

PRESENT. they were so very confidential together, behind the curtains.

(The group start making music, playing, singing, whistling. Exeunt, pulling off curtains.)

SCROOGE. Scrooge noticed that the Ghost was older, clearly older; its hair was gray. Are Spirit's lives so short?

PRESENT. My life upon this globe, is very brief. It ends tonight.

SCROOGE. Tonight! *(Fog appears.)*

PRESENT. Tonight at midnight. *(chimes)* Hark! The time is drawing near.

SCROOGE. Forgive me, but I see something strange, and not belonging to yourself, protruding from your skirts. Is it a foot or a claw!

PRESENT. It might be a claw, for the flesh there is upon it. Look here. From the folds of its robe, it brought two children: wretched, abject, frightful, miserable.

Oh, Man! look here. Look, look, down here! *(They are a boy and a girl, meager, scowling.)*

SCROOGE. Where angels might have sat enthroned, devils lurked and glared out menacing.

PRESENT. No change, no degradation, no perversion of humanity, in any grade, through all the mysteries of wonderful creation, has monsters half so horrible and dread.

SCROOGE. Spirit! Are they yours?

PRESENT. They are Man's. And they cling to me, appealing from their fathers. This boy is Ignorance. This girl is Want. Beware them both, but most of all beware this boy, for on his brow I see that written which is Doom, unless the writing be erased. *(bitterly)* Deny it! *(pointing towards the city)* Slander those who speak of it! Admit it for your factious purposes, and make it worse.

SCROOGE. Have they no refuge or resources?

PRESENT. Are there no prisons? Are there no workhouses? *(Exeunt)*

(The bell strikes twelve; the Ghost vanishes. Scrooge sees:)

SCROOGE. Remembering the prediction of old Jacob Marley, Scrooge saw a solemn phantom coming, like a mist along the ground. *(Fog.)*

STAVE FOUR: CHRISTMAS FUTURE
The Last of the Three Spirits

(Stave IV sign is brought on. Scrooge bends down upon his knee before the gloom and mystery)

SCROOGE. *(in dread)* I am in the presence of the Ghost of Christmas Yet To Come?

(The Spirit answers not, but points onward with its hand.)

SCROOGE. You are about to show me shadows of the things that have not happened, but will happen in the time before us. Is that so, Spirit?

(The robe which conceals the Spirit shows it has inclined its head.)

SCROOGE. Lead on! Lead on! The night is waning fast, and it is precious time to me, I know. Lead on, Spirit! *(Traveller opens to SLIDE No.10, MELAN-CHOLY LONDON)*

(The Spirit moves away. They are in the city. A funeral is in process; music. Four or five men enter, observing the coffin pass.)

　　- Well! Old Scratch has got his own at last, hey?

　　- So I see. Cold, isn't it?

- What has he done with his money?

- Left it to his Company, perhaps. He hasn't left it to *me*. That's all I know.

- It's likely to be a very cheap funeral. I don't know of anybody to go to it.

- Suppose we make up a party and follow the hearse.

- Is there to be lunch? I must be fed if I go. *(a laugh)*

SCROOGE. *(shuddering)* Spirit! I see, I see. The case of this unhappy man might be my own. My life tends that way now. *(He recoils in terror, for suddenly a corpse is carried on by four to six figures, the body under a sheet.)* Merciful Heaven, what is this! *(Scrooge looks wildly about him. The Phantom points to the head. A motion of Scrooge's finger would disclose the face.)*

CHORUS. Oh cold, cold, rigid dreadful Death, set up thine altar here: for this is thy dominion.

SCROOGE. No voice spoke and yet Scrooge heard these words.

CHORUS. He lies in the dark, empty house, with not a man, a woman, or a child, to say that he was kind to me, in this or that, and for the memory of one kind word I will be kind to him.

SCROOGE. Spirit! This is a fearful place. In leaving it, I shall not leave its lesson, trust me. Let us go!

(Still the Ghost points with unmoved finger to the head.)

SCROOGE. I understand you, and I would do it, if I could. But I have not the power, Spirit. I have not the power. (*CRATCHIT HOUSE SCRIM enters on wire.*

The Spirit spreads its dark robe like a wing; and withdrawing it reveals a room by daylight in Cratchit's house. The little children are still as statues; Peter is reading; the mother and her daughters are sewing.)

PETER. 'And He took a child, and set him in the midst of them.' (*He does not go on. The mother lays down her work and puts her hand up to her face.*)

MRS. CRATCHIT. The color hurts my eyes.

SCROOGE. The color? Ah, poor Tiny Tim!

MRS. CRATCHIT. They're better now again. Candlelight makes them weak; and I wouldn't show weak eyes to your father when he comes home, for the world. It must be near his time.

PETER. (*shutting his book*) Past it rather. But I think he's walked a little slower than he used, these few last evenings, mother.

(*They are very quiet again.*)

MRS. CRATCHIT. (*in a steady, cheerful voice, that only falters once*) I have known him walk with - I have known him walk with Tiny Tim upon his shoulder, very fast indeed.

PETER. And so have I. Often.

BELINDA. And so have I.

GIRL. So had all.

MRS. CRATCHIT. But he was very light to carry, *(intent on her work)* and his father loved him so, that it was no trouble - no trouble. And there is your father at the door! *(She hurries out to meet him. Bob enters in his comforter.)*

BELINDA. His tea was ready for him on the bob,

MARTHA. and they all tried who should help him to it most.

(The two young Cratchits get on his knees and each child lays a little cheek against his face.)

SCROOGE. As if they said, Don't mind it, Father. Don't be grieved!

CRATCHIT. Bob was very cheerful with them. *(looks at the work)* He praised the industry and speed of Mrs. Cratchit and the girls. They would be done before Sunday, he said.

MRS. CRATCHIT. Sunday! You went today then, Robert?

CRATCHIT. Yes, my dear. I wish you could have gone. It would have done you good to see how green a place it tis. But you'll see it often. I promised him that I would walk there on a Sunday. *(weeps)* My little child! My little child! *(Light on Tiny Tim, laid out behind scrim. Cratchit goes upstage behind the scrim, where Tiny Tim is laid out amidst Christmas decorations, sits in a chir, leans over and kisses the little face. He is reconciled. Returns.)* I am sure we shall none of us forget poor Tiny Tim - shall we - or this first parting that there was among us.

ALL. Never, Father!

CRATCHIT. And I know, my dears, that when we recollect how patient and mild he was; although he was a little, little child; we shall not quarrel easily among ourselves, and forget poor Tiny Tim in doing it.

ALL. No, never, Father.

CRATCHIT. I am very happy. I am very happy!

(Mrs. Cratchit kisses him, his daughters kiss him, the two young Cratchits kiss him, and he and Peter shake hands.)

SCROOGE. Spirit of Tiny Tim, thy childish essence was from God! Spectre, something informs me that our parting moment is at hand. I know it, but I know not how. Tell me what man that was whom we saw lying dead.

(The Spirit spreads its robe again like a wing: SLIDE No. 11, GRAVEYARD appears; traveller opens and they are in a graveyard; Spirit stands among the graves pointing down at one.)

SCROOGE. Before I draw nearer to that stone to which you point, answer me one question. Are these the shadows of the things that Will be, or are they shadows of things that May be, only? Men's courses will foreshadow certain ends, to which, if persevered in, they must lead. But if the courses be departed from, the ends will change. Say it is thus with what you show me!

(The finger points downward to the gravestone. Scrooge creeps towards it and reads his own name.)

SCROOGE. *Ebenezer Scrooge. (falls to his knees)* Am *I* that man who lay upon the bed? *(The finger points to him and back to the grave.)* No, Spirit! Oh, no, no! I am not the man I was. Why show me this, if I am past all hope? Good Spirit, your nature intercedes for me and pities me. Assure me that I may yet change these shadows you have shown me, by an altered life! *(The kind hand trembles.)* I will honor Christmas in my heart, and try to keep it all the year. I will live in the Past, Present, and the Future. I will not shut out the lessons that they teach. Oh, tell me I may sponge away the writing on this stone! *(In his agony he grasps the spectral hand, which tries to free itself and does. Scrooge holds up his hands in a last prayer, and sees the Phantom change.)* It shrunk, collapsed, and dwindled down into a bedpost. *(GRAVEYARD SLIDE out as scene ends.)*

STAVE FIVE: THE END OF IT

(Players bring Stave V sign onstage. SLIDE No. 12: CHRISTMAS MORN.)

SCROOGE. Yes! And the bedpost was his own, the room was his own. Best and happiest of all, the Time before him was his own, to make amends in! Oh Jacob Marley! Heaven, and the Christmas Time be praised for this. I say it on my knees, old Jacob, on my knees! *(trying to dress, laughing and crying at once)* I don't know what to do! I am as merry as a schoolboy. I am as giddy as a drunken man. A merry Christmas to everybody! A happy New Year to all the world! I don't know how long I've been among the Spirits. I don't know anything. I'm quite a baby. Never mind. I don't care. *(A lusty peal of bells is heard; goes to window and calls down to a boy.)* What's today?

BOY. Eh?

SCROOGE. What's today, my fine fellow?

BOY. Today! Why, CHRISTMAS DAY.

SCROOGE. It's Christmas Day. I haven't missed it. The Spirits have done it all in one night. Hallo, my fine fellow.

BOY. Hallo!

SCROOGE. Do you know the poulterer's, in the next street but one, at the corner?

BOY. I should hope I did.

SCROOGE. An intelligent boy! Do you know whether they've sold the prize turkey that was hanging up there? The big one.

BOY. What, the one as big as me?

SCROOGE. What a delightful boy. It's a pleasure to talk to him. Yes, my buck!

BOY. It's hanging there now.

SCROOGE. Is it? Go and buy it.

BOY. Walker-ER!

SCROOGE. No, no. I am in earnest. Go and buy it and tell 'em to bring it here that I may give them directions where to take it. Come back with the man and I'll give you a shilling. *(the boy is off like a shot)* I'll send it to Bob Cratchit's! *(rubbing his hands and laughing)* He shan't know who sends it. It's twice the size of Tiny Tim. *(writes address down and goes to door)* I shall love this knocker as long as I live. *(pats it)* What an honest expression on its face. Here's the turkey. Hallo! Whoop! *(to man)* Merry Christmas! How are you!

MAN. *(under the weight)* It *was* a turkey! He never could have stood on his legs, that bird.

BOY. He would have snapped 'em short off in a minute,

MAN. like sticks of sealing wax.

SCROOGE.   Why, it's impossible to carry that to Cratchit's, you must have a cab. *(reaches into pocket to pay for everything)* Then he went to church, and walked about the streets, and patted children on the head, and questioned beggars, and found that everything could yield him pleasure. *(walks with hands behind his back, a delighted smile on his face. Passerby respond to him.)*

PASSERS. Good morning, sir! A merry Christmas to you!

SCROOGE. Scrooge said often afterwards, that of all the blithe sounds he had ever heard, those were the blithest in his ears. In the afternoon he turned his steps towards his nephew's house. He passed the door a dozen times before he had the courage to knock. *(to maid)* Is your master at home, my dear? Nice girl! Very.

MAID. Yes, sir.

SCROOGE. Where is he my love?

MAID. He's in the dining room, sir, along with the mistress. I'll show you upstairs, if you please.

SCROOGE. Thank'ee. He knows me, *(in the entrance)* I'll go in here, my dear. *(enters)* Fred! *(the wife is startled)*

FRED. Why bless my soul! Who's that?

SCROOGE. It's I. Your uncle Scrooge. I have come to dinner. Will you let me in, Fred?

FRED. Let him in! It is a mercy he didn't shake his arm off!

SCROOGE. He was at home in five minutes. Nothing could be heartier.

WIFE. His niece looked just the same.

TOPPER. So did Topper when *he* came.

PLUMP GIRL. So did the plump sister, when *she* came.

OTHERS. So did everyone when *they* came.

FRED. Wonderful party,

WIFE. wonderful games,

OTHERS. wonderful unanimity,

TOPPER & PLUMP GIRL. won-der-ful happiness! *(exeunt omnes)*

SCROOGE. But he was early at the office next morning. If he could only be there first, and catch Bob Cratchit coming late! The clock struck nine. No Bob. A quarter past. No Bob. He was a full eighteen minutes and a half behind his time. *(Scrooge has his door open.)*

CRATCHIT. His hat was off, before he opened the door; his comforter too. He was on his stool in a jiffy; driving away with his pen as of he were trying to overtake nine o'clock.

SCROOGE. Hallo! What do you mean by coming here at this time of day?

CRATCHIT. I am very sorry, sir, I *am* behind my time.

SCROOGE. You are? Yes, I think you are. Step this way, if you please.

CRATCHIT. It's only once a year, sir. It shall not be repeated. I was making rather merry yesterday, sir.

SCROOGE. Now, I'll tell you what, my friend. I am not going to stand this sort of thing any longer. And therefore, *(leaps from his stool and digs Cratchit in the waistcoat so he staggers back to the Tank)* and therefore I am about to raise your salary!

CRATCHIT. *(Thinks of getting the ruler and knocking Scrooge down with it, and sending for the strait jacket.)*

SCROOGE. A merry Christmas, Bob! *(clapping him on the back)* A merrier Christmas, Bob, my good fellow, than I have given you, for many a year! I'll raise your salary, and endeavor to assist your struggling family, and we will discuss your affairs this very afternoon, over a Christmas bowl of smoking bishop. Bob! Make up the fires, and buy another coal-scuttle before you dot another i, Bob Cratchit!

(Chorus sings 'Joy to the World,' one verse. All of Cratchit's family enters and sings.)

CRATCHIT. Scrooge was better than his word. He did it all and infinitely more;

MARTHA. and to Tiny Tim,

GIRL. who did NOT die,

MARTHA. he was a second father.

MRS. CRATCHIT. He became as good a friend, and as good a man, as the good old city knew,

PETER. or any other good old city, town, or borough,

BOY. in the good old world.

SCROOGE. Some people laughed to see the alteration in him, but he let them laugh, and little heeded them; for he was wise enough to know that nothing ever happened on this globe, for good, at which some people did not have their fill of laughter. His own heart laughed: and that was quite enough for him.

MRS. CRATCHIT. and it was always said of him, that he knew how to keep Christmas well,

CRATCHIT. if any man alive possessed the knowledge.

BELINDA. May that be truly said of us, and all of us!

PETER. And so, as Tiny Tim observed,

TINY TIM. God bless us, Every One!

CURTAIN

THEATER GAMES
FOR STORY THEATER

by Viola Spolin

Story Theater is a way to tell myths, legends, folk and fairy tales as well as history and literature with theatrical integrity. Players, who both tell the story and play the character, work in open space which they shape to show the natural world, helpin for Story Theater may be found in Paul Sill'sg the audience see the invisible. Shadow screens, projections, curtains and music assist the transformation, as well as vocal sound effects and minimal lighting, with only the occasional need for blocks or ramps to give height or a touch of abstraction to a set.

These Theater Games introduces players to space and space objects and will generate trust and a spirit of play within your group. The traditional games included here may be played as warmups to sessions or whenever energy levels begin to fall within a rehearsal.

The trap for most beginners, child or adult, is "in the head" acting. To escape the trap there must be focus. The games will give players experience of focus that can free them from their ideas of acting and make real what it means to tell a story on stage.

Viola Spolin, 1970

Additional Theater Games may be found in *Paul Sills' Story Theater: Four Shows* (Applause, 2000)

FEELING SELF WITH SELF:

Focus: on feeling self with self.

This exercise, which gives players a full body perception of self, can follow a traditional game to start workshops and may be used frequently, alone or leading into a **Space Walk**.

Description: Entire group sits quietly. Players physically feel what is against their bodies with their bodies as side coached. Side coach continuously. If necessary, coach players to keep their eyes open.

Side Coaching: **Feel your self with your self! Feel your feet with your feet! Feel your feet in your stockings and your stockings on your feet! Feel your slacks or skirt on your legs and your legs in your slacks or skirt! Feel your underclothing next to your body and your body next to your underclothing! Feel your shirt against your chest and your chest inside your shirt! Feel your ring on your finger and your finger in your ring! Feel the hair on your head! Your eyebrows on your forehead! Feel your nose against your cheeks! Your ears! Your tongue inside your mouth! Try to feel the inside of your head with your head! Feel all the space around you! Now let the space feel you!**

Evaluation: Was there a difference between feeling your ring on your finger and feeling your finger in the ring?

SPACE WALKS AND SPACE SHAPING:

Introduction

Space Walks and **Space Shaping** exercises are ways of perceiving/sensing/experiencing the environment (space) around us as an actual dimension in which all can enter, communicate, live and be free. Each player becomes a receiving/sending instrument capable of reaching out beyond the physical self and the immediate environment. As water supports and surrounds marine life, space substance surrounds and supports us. Objects made of space substance may be looked upon as thrusts/projections of the (invisible) inner self into the visible world, intuitively perceived/sensed as a manifest phenomenon, *real!* When the invisible (not yet emerged, inside, unknown) becomes visible - seen and perceived - theater magic! This is the fertile ground of the poet, the artist, the seeker.

SPACE WALK #1 (EXPLORATION):

Focus: on feeling space with the whole body.

Description: Players move around and physically investigate space as an unknown substance. Leader walks with players during side coaching.

Side Coaching: **Move through the substance and make contact with it! Use your whole body to make contact! Feel it against your cheeks! Your nose! Your knees! Your hips! Let it (space) feel you! Feel your body shape as you move through it!** (If players tend to use hands only, coach: **Let your hands be as one with the rest of your body! Move as a single mass!**) **Explore the substance! You never felt it before! Make a tunnel! Move back into the space your body has shaped! Shake it up! Make it fly! Make it ripple! Eyes open!**

SPACE WALK #2 (SUPPORT AND EFFORT)

Focus: on letting space support you or holding yourself together as side coached.

Description: Players walk around, moving through the space substance, open to the side coaching. After the players are responding to the support of space, coach them to support themselves. Then, coach players to go back to letting space support them. Calling out parts of the body helps to release muscle holds. Change back and forth until the difference between space support and holding self together is realized by players.

Side Coaching: A: **As you walk, let the space substance support you! Rest on it! Lean into it! Let it support your head! Your chin! Your eyeballs! Your upper lip, etc.!** *B*: **Now, you are your sole support! As you walk, you are holding yourself together! Your face! Your arms! Your whole skeleton! If you quit holding yourself together, you would fly into a thousand pieces! You are hanging onto your arms! Your mouth! Your forehead** (calling out that which is held rigid)**! Note what you feel when you are your sole support!** *C*: **Now change! Walk through the space and let the space support you! Don't worry about what that means! Your body will understand! Let the space take over where you were holding! Note your body feeling! Let the space support you! Let space support your eyes! Your face! Your shoulders! Your upper lip! You go through the space and let the space go through you!** (Continue to change back and forth between support and effort until players experience the difference.)

Evaluation: To players: How did you feel when space was supporting you? When you were your own support? To audience: Did you perceive a difference between support and no support in the way players walked and looked?

Point of Observation:
   When players hold themselves together, are their own gravity line, so to speak, some shrink up, some seem to be afraid of falling, while others appear anxious, lonely and still others look aggressive. In fact, many 'character qualities' appear. When, on the other hand, players lean on space, an expansiveness and fullness can be noted as they move through the environment. It is as if they knew the environment will support them if they allow it to.

SPACE WALK #3 (SKELETON)
(Warm Up: **Space Walk** #1, #2)

Focus: on physical movement of one's skeleton in space.

Description: Full group. Players walk through space focusing on skeletal movement of bones and joints.

Side Coaching: **You go through the space and let the space go through you! Feel your skeleton moving in space! Avoid seeing a picture of your skeleton! Feel your skeleton with your skeleton! Feel the movement of every joint! Allow your joints to move freely! Observe where you are interfering! But don't do anything about it! And don't not do anything about it! Feel the movement of your spine! Your pelvic bones! Your leg bones! Let your head rest on its own pedestal! Feel your skull with your skull! Now put space where your brains are! Where your cheeks are!**

Around your arm bones! Between each disc in your spinal column! Put space where your stomach is! But hang on to your skeleton! Feel your skeleton moving in the space! Heighten the movement of your joints! Feel your own form once more! The outer outline of your whole body in space! Feel where the space ends and you begin! You walk through the space and let space through you! Take note of your skeleton moving in space! Everybody close your eyes! When I call "Open your eyes!", you will be in a new place! Now, open your eyes! See the new place you are in! (Repeat this 2 or 3 times.) **Your next step is into an unknown place! You are now stepping into an unknown place!**

Evaluation: Did you begin to get the feeling of your own skeleton in space?

Points of Observation:

1. Younger children who may be put off by the word 'skeleton' should be made aware of the fact that the skeleton is the basic frame of every person's body. This exercise will help.

2. When body space is connected to outer space in this exercise, some players can experience anxiety. Should anxiety appear at this point, bring players back to their own body form quickly.

DESIGNING FOR STORY THEATER
by Carol Bleackley

In all stories the space transforms from cottage to castle, ground to sky, through the forest to under the sea and this must be shown by players with the help of lighting and changes in stage color, height and shape.

SHADOW SCREENS and SHADOW PLAY:

Spolin's space walks will help the company relax bodily holds, flow through space and shape it as if it were a substance so they can play onstage, without scenery or props. A genuine visual effect is possible with the use of shadows and projection of colored gels onto a playing area and shadow screen, changing with the story's transformations.

For instance, screens 4' or 5' wide x 8' tall surround a center screen 10' wide by 8' tall and are each backlit by 150 watt lamps on dimmers controlled by the lighting person. The stage muslin is stretched onto frames made of two by fours. The screens must be screwed into the stage floor and anchored from behind the top to the walls. Masking is used as necessary. The players closely move behind the screens; their shadows appearing when the screens are backlit. When onstage, players work with space substance objects, but when in shadow use real props to show objects. Thus, Simpleton may carry a cut-out cardboard goose shape when in shadow but emerge onstage carrying a space goose. The audience is delighted by this. Any offstage event can be shown this way. Clever Gretel preparing the chicken, feathers flying, cleaver swinging, followed by her entrance with a space chicken on a space spit. Another player or players on a mike provide sound effects.

By playing with the shadows, experimenting with the height of the light sources for the screens, we have filled the screens with the lower half of giants, and amplified their voices. Players become adept at finding shadow images for their parts. Long entrances or exits on two or three screens can be effective. A platform behind the screens to raise the action a few inches helps to show the full figure.

PLAYS FOR PERFORMANCE

Rights Available from Applause

A Critic and His Wife
Amazon All-Stars
The Bug
Bunny, Bunny
A Christmas Carol
The Contest
The Custom of the Country
Cyrano de Bergerac
Date with a Stranger
The Day the Bronx Died
Dear
Ghost in the Machine
I Am A Man
Little Red Riding Hood
The Mothers
Night Baseball
The Paul Sill's Story Theater
The Postcard
Pinocchio
The Scarlet Letter
Senior Square
The Valentine Fairy
Zipless
and many more!

PAUL SILLS'
STORY THEATER:
Four Shows

Adapted for the stage
by Paul Sills

Including essays and introductions by
Paul Sills on directing for *Story Theater*
and
**A Special Section: Theatre Games for
Story Theater by Viola Spolin**

The creator of Story Theater, the original
director of Second City, and one of the great
popularizers of improvisational theater, Paul Sills
has assembled some of his favorite adaptations
from world literature:

The Blue Light And Other Stories
A Christmas Carol - Charles Dickens
Stories of God - Rainer Maria Rilke
Rumi - Jalalludin Rumi

CLOTH•ISBN 1-55783-398-2 • $26.95